TABLE OF CONTENTS

Big Air   4

A Natural   10

Future Boy   14

Two-Sport Star   19

In the Spotlight   24

Selected Career Highlights   30
Glossary   31
Further Reading & Websites   31
Index   32

Shaun gets ready for his first run.

BIG AIR

Snowboarder Shaun White was fighting for
the gold medal in the Men's **Halfpipe** event.
He was at the 2010 Winter **Olympic Games** in

Revised Edition

Shaun White

By Matt Doeden

AMAZING ATHLETES

Lerner Publications Company • Minneapolis

Lerner Publications Company
A division of Lerner Publishing Group, Inc.
241 First Avenue North
Minneapolis, MN 55401 USA

For reading levels and more information, look up this title at www.lernerbooks.com.

Library of Congress Cataloging-in-Publication Data

Doeden, Matt.
   Shaun White / By Matt Doeden. — Rev. ed.
       p.   cm. — (Amazing athletes)
   Includes bibliographical references and index.
   ISBN 978-0-7613-6859-5 (lib. bdg. : alk. paper)
   ISBN 978-0-7613-6860-1 (eBook)
   1. White, Shaun, 1986– 2. Snowboarders—United States—Biography—Juvenile literature. I. Title.
GV857.S57D633 2011
796.939092—dc22 [B]   2010011042

Manufactured in the United States of America
3 – HF – 4/1/14

Vancouver, Canada. Shaun did well on his **qualifying run**. He got **big air** and landed all of his **tricks**. His score of 46.8 was the best of the first round. Snowboarder after snowboarder tried to beat Shaun's score. But no one could match it.

Fans cheer for Shaun during the halfpipe event.

As he got ready for his final run on the halfpipe, the pressure was off. He knew he had already won the gold medal. But Shaun always puts on a good show. He didn't want to

Shaun soars through the air during his qualifying run.

disappoint the crowd. Thousands of fans were in the stands. Millions more were watching on TV. "I wanted a victory lap that would be remembered," Shaun said.

Shaun was the last snowboarder to take his second run. His "victory lap" was the most exciting run of the night. He soared higher and spun faster than the other snowboarders. Shaun was having fun. For his final trick, Shaun tried the **Double McTwist 1260**. This is a very dangerous move. It has three and a half twists. They are followed by two head-over-heels flips. No one had ever tried this trick in Olympic competition before.

Snowboarding was included as an Olympic sport for the first time in 1998. The Winter Games were held that year in Nagano, Japan.

Shaun takes his "victory lap" on the halfpipe.

As he soared through the air, Shaun spun and twisted as fast as he could. He got his snowboard beneath him just before crashing into the snow. Shaun landed the trick! "I can't even describe what it feels like," Shaun said after nailing the Double

McTwist 1260. "I think about how many times I have done that run in my mind, and to land it here feels incredible."

Shaun's final-run score of 48.4 was the highest of the event. He had won the gold medal. No one would ever forget his amazing performance. Finland's Peetu Piiroinen finished in second place. "It's impossible to beat Shaun unless he falls," Piiroinen said after the competition.

One of Shaun's supporters is snowboarding legend and designer Jake Burton. He was in the crowd in Vancouver to watch Shaun's incredible feat. "With a gold medal already in his pocket, Shaun went out and beat his winning score," Burton said after the event. "What a testament to how much fun snowboarding is. And what a true champion Shaun is."

Shaun grew up in Carlsbad, California, a suburb of San Diego.

A Natural

The life of the future Olympic champion got off to a rough start. Shaun Roger White was born September 3, 1986, in San Diego, California. He was not a healthy baby. He had a heart condition called **tetralogy of Fallot**. The condition affected the oxygen supply in Shaun's blood. His parents, Cathy and Roger, had to bring Shaun in for two heart surgeries when he was very young. After the surgeries, Cathy couldn't even hold her infant son. Instead, she just held on to Shaun's tiny feet.

Shaun recovered and grew into an energetic boy. He was always on the go. He loved to surf, ski, jump on a trampoline, and play soccer. He looked up to his older brother, Jesse, and did his best to keep up.

Shaun's brother, Jesse, works for Burton Snowboards (a popular snowboarding company). He helps manage all the riders Burton sponsors. He also works with Shaun to design new snowboards and clothing.

One hobby the brothers shared was skateboarding. They spent hours learning simple tricks on the small ramp in their backyard. The family also took trips to a skiing resort at Bear Mountain in California. There, little Shaun tore down the slopes on his skis.

By the age of six, Shaun had become fascinated with the snowboarders at Bear Mountain. He wanted to learn how to ride. But

Bear Mountain is a popular skiing spot in California. Shaun admired the snowboarders there.

the resort wouldn't give lessons to anyone younger than 12. Shaun's father wanted to encourage his son. So Roger took lessons and taught Shaun how to snowboard.

Shaun's mom worried about her son. Snowboarding seemed dangerous. She told Shaun that he was only allowed to ride **fakie**. She hoped that making him ride backward would slow him down.

It didn't work. Shaun was a snowboarding natural. From the start, he was comfortable on the board. In 1993, at the age of seven, he won his first **amateur** snowboarding contest. With the win, Shaun got to compete in the 12-and-under division of the United States Amateur Snowboard Association (USASA) National Championships. Shaun took 11th place. His career was off to a fast start.

Shaun's ability to get big air helped him win many trophies.

FUTURE BOY

Shaun's growing skills earned him plenty of attention. He was easily the best snowboarder in his age group. He won trophy after trophy during competitions in the mid- and late 1990s. His ability to land difficult tricks and get big air helped him win five national titles in the 12-and-under division.

"I first saw [Shaun] snowboarding when he was about nine," said skateboarding legend Tony Hawk. "He was just this little pixie with a giant helmet, coming down the halfpipe. Now, he's grown into his own style—plus he can do tricks five feet higher than everyone else."

Skateboarder Tony Hawk (*left*) was impressed with Shaun's snowboarding skills.

Snowboarding wasn't Shaun's only passion. He was also becoming a skilled skateboarder. "I think that skateboarding was a way for me to kind of keep the same feeling going during the summertime," he said.

"I don't live in the mountains, and I don't constantly think about snowboarding. If I did, I would get tired of it. I'm in it all winter. By the time snowboarding is almost over, skateboarding is the light at the end of the tunnel. . . . By the time [summer is] over, all I can think about is getting back on the snow."

Despite his great success, Shaun's snowboarding was tough on his family. As an amateur, he didn't earn any prize money for his riding. His parents spent as much as $20,000 per year on equipment, travel, and other expenses. The family often slept in their

During summers in California, Shaun would go skateboarding.

van because they couldn't afford a hotel room.

In 2000, 13-year-old Shaun decided to change that. He left the world of amateur snowboarding and turned **professional**. As a pro, he could earn money in competitions and for **endorsements**. Burton Snowboards quickly signed the young star to his first endorsement deal. His family's money problems were solved.

The Winter X Games and the Summer X Games are events that focus on "extreme" sports. The Winter X Games include events such as snowboarding and skiing. At the Summer X Games, athletes compete in surfing and skateboarding competitions, among other events.

Turning pro was a big step for such a young athlete. But Shaun quickly proved that he belonged alongside the best snowboarders in the world. He earned the nickname Future Boy. Fans and snowboarders alike could see that he was the future of the sport.

Shaun flies during the Winter X Games.

TWO-SPORT STAR

By 2002, Shaun was no longer just the future of the sport. He had arrived. But even though he had a great year, the 15-year-old kept coming up just a little bit short. He tried to qualify for the U.S. Winter Olympic team. But he missed the cut by 0.3 points. At the Winter X Games, he finished second in both the **slopestyle** and **superpipe** events.

Tony Hawk *(left)* helped Shaun *(right)*
become a professional skateboarder.

That summer, Shaun focused more on his skateboarding. He joined Tony Hawk's Gigantic Skatepark Tour. He rode with and learned from the best skateboarders in the world. Tony Hawk encouraged Shaun to become a professional skateboarder. It was an interesting idea. But first Shaun wanted to concentrate on the 2003 snowboarding season.

It was a good decision. In 2003, Shaun dominated his competitors with huge moves. At the Winter X Games, he took gold in both the slopestyle and superpipe events. He also became the youngest rider to win the U.S. Open Slopestyle Championship. Shaun ended the season as the world's top-ranked snowboarder.

Shaun rides high to win gold medals at the 2003 Winter X Games.

Shaun enjoyed his success in snowboarding. But the idea of becoming a professional skateboarder stuck with him. He ended his 2003 snowboarding season early to get ready for his first skateboarding event as a pro. A few weeks later, Shaun finished fourth in the **vert** competition at the 2003 Slam City Jam North American Skateboarding Championships in Vancouver, Canada.

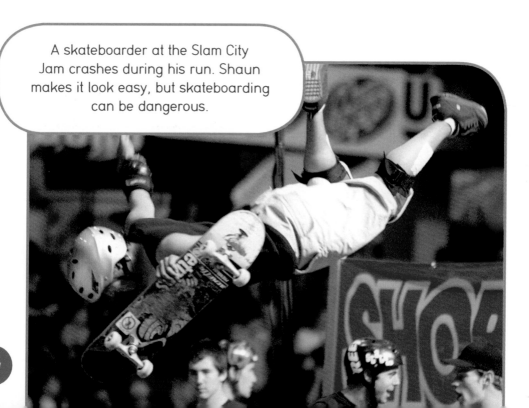

A skateboarder at the Slam City Jam crashes during his run. Shaun makes it look easy, but skateboarding can be dangerous.

The next big event for Shaun was the Summer X Games. He took sixth place in the vert competition. This was a great result for someone who spent most of his time snowboarding. For his performance in both snowboarding and skateboarding, Shaun won the ESPN "Espy" award for Best Action Sports Athlete. He had arrived as one of the biggest stars in extreme sports.

Shaun won his second gold medal in slopestyle at the 2004 Winter X Games.

IN THE SPOTLIGHT

Shaun was on top of the world. And he was still just 17 years old! What would he do next? All eyes were on him at the 2004 Winter X Games. He was trying to repeat his double-gold effort of 2003. But after his qualifying run, Shaun felt a sharp pain in his knee. He couldn't continue.

Shaun had surgery to repair the damaged knee that spring. He was feeling better in time for the 2005 Winter X Games. He won the slopestyle event for the third time in three years. Shaun took silver in skateboarding vert at the 2005 Summer X Games. With the second-place finish, he became the first athlete to win a medal in both the Summer and the Winter X Games.

Shaun won his first Summer X Games medal in 2005.

Shaun won two more gold medals at the 2006 Winter X Games. By this time, he had established himself as the best snowboarder in the world. He was named to the U.S. Winter Olympic team for the 2006 games in Torino, Italy. He had the best score in the Men's Halfpipe event and took home the gold medal.

The White family *(from left)*—Cathy, Kari, Shaun, Jesse, and Roger—celebrates Shaun's gold medal in 2006.

Shaun appeared on *The Tonight Show with Jay Leno* in March 2010.

"It's the best year of my life," he said. "I don't think I'll ever have this again. It's amazing."

Shaun's Olympic gold was the highlight of one of the most successful snowboarding seasons in history. Fans wanted to meet him. Reporters wanted to interview him. The attention didn't let up as Shaun won X Games medals in 2007, 2008, 2009, and 2010. Shaun's gold medal at the 2010 Winter Olympics made him more popular than ever. He even appeared on *The Tonight Show with Jay Leno.*

Shaun enjoys the attention. With endorsements and other projects, he makes millions of dollars each year. He has a snowboarding DVD called *The White Album*. He's appeared in a TV program called *First Descent*. His clothing line, called Shaun White 4 Target, and video game—*Shaun White Snowboarding: Road Trip*—sell well.

Shaun has had a lot of success. But he was just 23 years old at the 2010 Winter Olympics. The next Winter Games will be held in 2014 in Sochi, Russia. With Shaun's passion for the sport as strong as ever,

In 2009, Shaun and his brother designed a room at Target House. This is a place to stay for people receiving long-term care at St. Jude Children's Research Hospital. The "Shaun White Great Room" is a place to hang out and meet new friends.

fans can look forward to another amazing Olympic performance.

Shaun proudly shows off his gold medal in Vancouver.

Selected Career Highlights

2011 Won the ESPN "Espy" award for Best Action Sports Athlete

2010 Won a gold medal in the halfpipe competition at the Winter Olympics in Vancouver, Canada
Won his third straight gold in superpipe at the Winter X Games

2009 Won his second straight gold in superpipe at the Winter X Games

2008 Won a gold medal in superpipe at the Winter X Games

2007 Won a gold medal in skateboarding vert at the Summer X Games

2006 Won a gold medal in the halfpipe competition at the Winter Olympics in Torino, Italy
Won his fourth straight gold in slopestyle at the Winter X Games

2005 Qualified for the U.S. Winter Olympic team
Won a silver medal in skateboarding vert to become the first athlete to earn a medal in both the Summer and Winter X Games
Won his first skateboarding gold in the vert event on the Dew Action Sports Tour
Won his third straight gold in slopestyle at the Winter X Games

2004 Released his snowboarding DVD, *The White Album*
Won gold in slopestyle at the Winter X Games

2003 Took part in his first Summer X Games, placing sixth in skateboarding vert
Won his first gold medals at the Winter X Games in slopestyle and superpipe
Won the ESPN "Espy" award for Best Action Sports Athlete

2002 Took home two silver medals from the Winter X Games with second-place finishes in both slopestyle and superpipe

2001 Finished in the top ten in the slopestyle and superpipe events at the Winter X Games

2000 Accepted his first endorsement deal with Burton Snowboards

1993 Won his first amateur snowboarding competition

Glossary

amateur: an athlete who does not receive money to compete in events

Double McTwist 1260: a move on a snowboard that has three and a half twists and two head-over-heels flips

endorsements: deals in which an athlete gets money to promote companies' products

fakie: riding a snowboard backward

halfpipe: a long, U-shaped ramp

Olympic Games: an event held every four years in which athletes from around the world compete in dozens of different sports

professional: an athlete who is paid to compete in events

qualifying run: the first run in a snowboard or skateboard competition

slopestyle: a snowboarding competition in which riders do tricks over a series of jumps

superpipe: a snowboarding competition in which riders do tricks on a large halfpipe

tetralogy of Fallot: a heart problem that affects the supply of oxygen in the blood

tricks: spins, loops, flips, and other moves that are scored by judges

vert: a skateboarding competition held on a U-shaped vertical ramp

Further Reading & Websites

Barr, Matt, and Chris Moran. *Snowboarding.* Minneapolis: Lerner Publications Company, 2004.

ESPN.com
http://espn.go.com/action
ESPN.com's page devoted to extreme sports has updates on many sports, including snowboarding and skateboarding.

United States Olympic Committee
http://www.usoc.org/26_38188.htm
Read a profile of Shaun White on the official website of the United States Olympic Committee.

Index

Bear Mountain, California, 12
Burton Snowboards, 11, 17

Dew Action Sports Tour,
Double McTwist 1260, 7–9

"Espy" award, 23

First Descent, 28

Gold medal, 4, 6, 9, 21, 26–27, 29

Hawk, Tony, 15, 20

Men's Halfpipe, 4–5, 26

"Shaun White Great Room", 28
Shaun White Snowboarding: Road
 Trip, 28
Shaun White 4 Target, 28
skateboarding, 12, 16–17, 20, 22, 25
Slam City Jam North American
 Skateboarding Championships,
 22

Summer X Games, 16, 23, 25

Tonight Show with Jay Leno, The, 27
Tony Hawk's Gigantic Skatepark
 Tour, 20

United States Amateur Snowboard Association (USASA), 13
U.S. Open Slopestyle Championship, 21

White, Jesse (brother), 11, 26, 28
White, Cathy (mother), 11, 13, 26
White, Roger (father), 11, 13, 26
White, Shaun: birth of, 10–11;
 childhood of, 11–13 ; and en-
 dorsements, 17, 28 ; and learn-
 ing to snowboard, 13–14 ;
 nicknames, 18 ; and popularity
 of, 14, 18, 21, 23, 26–27
White Album, The, 28
Winter Olympic Games, 4, 27–28
Winter Olympic team, 19, 26
Winter X Games, 7, 19, 21, 24–26

Photo Acknowledgments

The images in this book are used with the permission of: © Streeter Lecka/
Getty Images, p. 4; Paul Drinkwater/NBCU Photo Bank via AP Images, pp. 5,
27; © Martin Bureau/AFP/Getty Images, p. 6; AP Photo/Sean Kilpatrick,
CP, p. 8; © Sam Wells - swellsphoto.com, p. 10; © Bob Rowan, Progressive
Image/CORBIS, p. 12; © Kevin Zacher, p. 14; © Tom Hauck/Getty Images,
p. 15; © Tim Rue/CORBIS, pp. 17, 20; © Al Bello/Getty Images, p. 19;
© Donald Miralle/Getty Images, p. 21; REUTERS/Andy Clark, p. 22; © Kevin
Winter/Getty Images, p. 23; © Jed Jacobsohn/Getty Images, p. 24; © Nick
Laham/Getty Images, p. 25; © Mike Powell/Getty Images, p. 26; © Kevork
Djansezian/Getty Images, p. 29; © Adam Pretty/Getty Images, p. 30.

Front Cover: AP Photo/Bela Szandelszky.